NARRO [illegible] VENTURE

John Poole

First published in 1975
by
Thornhill Press

ISBN 0 904110 10 9

Printed by Albert E. Smith (Printers) Ltd., Longsmith Street, Gloucester.

NARROW BOAT VENTURE

by

JOHN POOLE

The folded map of the whole of the waterways system was published in 1974 by the British Waterways Board and is included with their authority and approval.

Thornhill Press
7 Russell St.
Gloucester

FOREWORD

In this age of " built in depreciation " coupled with the " throw away cult " it is refreshing to read of the restoration of Barrhead originally built in 1937 as a G.U.C.C.C. butty. Whilst possibly not a true object of great beauty, a narrow boat is extremely functional and possesses a ponderous majesty and grace. Jeremy and Philip are to be congratulated on their skill and ingenuity.

In describing his voyages on the Oxford, Llangollen and Grand Union Canals, and the River Thames, the author kindly pays tribute to the work of the Inland Waterways Association. This voluntary and charitable body has fought strenuously for years for the retention of the waterways system for amenity use at a time when the policy of the Authorities was for abandonment and obliteration. It is now universally accepted that the canals are a priceless asset for recreation, but although the principle has been accepted by the Authorities, the necessary finance has not been made available to restore the network into a fully satisfactory condition. The backlog of maintenance is mentioned in the book and although the British Waterways Board are making considerable efforts to improve conditions they are sadly hampered by a shortage of cash.

Holiday cruises as described in this book are becoming increasingly popular with many people and to increase the variety and the range the Inland Waterways Association are actively engaged in restoring closed and abandoned canals. Money is raised through the Association's Restoration Fund and used to pay for work done by the I.W.A. and by enthusiastic volunteers who join working parties operating all over the country in the actual physical repair work. Major successes achieved this year are the opening of the Upper Avon to Stratford, the Ashton and Lower Peak Forest Canals and the Caldon Canal. Work is proceeding on many more including the Kennet and Avon, Montgomeryshire and Droitwich Canals.

We still need more support and I hope the readers of this book, if they approve our aims, will join the Association and write to 114, Regents Park Road, London, NW1 8UQ for details. Mr. Poole describes his odyssey to Inglesham above Lechlade on the River

Thames and wistfully regrets he cannot cruise back to Stroud by way of the Thames and Severn Canal through Sapperton Tunnel. Why indeed should he not ? The Inland Waterways Association does not feel that any navigation restoration is impossible, providing we are given sufficient support. We do need, however, more help in our work, as we must obtain sufficient finance both private and from Government and Local Authorities and this can only be achieved by increasing public demands for our objectives.

I am sure John Poole and his family will have many more trips and adventures in Barrhead and hope that their experiences will warn readers of the care necessary on the tidal waters of the lower Thames.

Wilmslow,
February, 1975

J. C. HEAP,
Chairman, Inland Waterways Association.

BARRHEAD

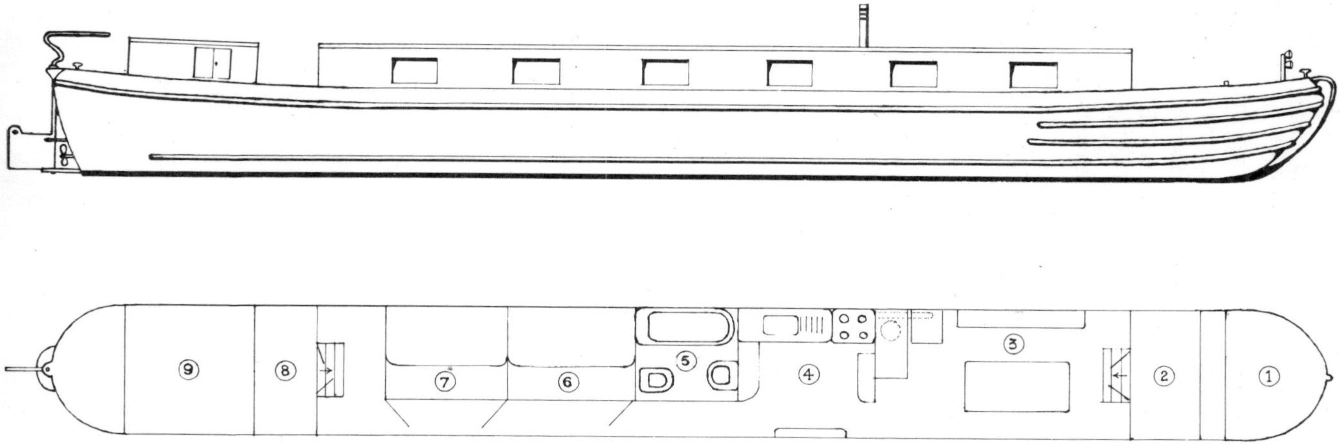

1. **FOREPEAK** housing 250 gall. water tank.
2. **FORWARD WELL DECK** with seat/locker housing gas cylinders (vented to atmosphere).
3. **SALOON** with central heating boiler, hot water tank in airing cupboard.
4. **GALLEY** with gas cooker, sink and drainer.
5. **BATHROOM** with bath, basin, radiator, chemical toilet.
6. **CABIN** with upper and lower double berths, double berth under after well deck, radiator.
7. **AFTER WELL DECK.**
8. **ENGINE HOUSING FORD 4D** diesel engine, fuel tanks, stand-by diesel generating set.

NARROW BOAT VENTURE

This story of the conversion of the narrow boat Barrhead and the account of some of her subsequent travels has been written mainly for the interest of the many thousands of men and women who have a lively concern for the country's canals and rivers and the craft which travel upon them. It is hoped that others will also read the story and that they will be encouraged to join with these dedicated enthusiasts in their labours to restore and preserve this neglected but valuable part of our national heritage.

Barrhead is jointly owned by my son Jeremy and son-in-law Philip, who also carried out her conversion. During the summer I was invited to join them and their families for a holiday exploring some of the more distant parts of the waterway system. Roughly 600 miles of canal and river were covered in a period of some twenty weeks, the later stages at week-ends as business commitments permitted.

The actual conversion took over three years to complete and entailed much hard work and a great deal of resourcefulness combined with skill and ingenuity to keep the cost within reasonable bounds. To this end, a heavy duty diesel-powered arc-welding set was hired for the early work on the hull and this, combined with the use of their own oxy-acetelene cutting equipment, meant that they were mostly independent of outside help.

Their estimate of cost—disregarding their own labour—was £1,200, probably less than one quarter of what it would have been had the project been carried out commercially with a new engine and gearbox and other large items of equipment. The work was done almost entirely in the Victoria Basin of the Gloucester Docks, where the converters were fortunate to be granted the facilities of a quay-side workshop. Here, various plant and power points for portable tools were available.

The lay-out and much of the construction were based on experience gained by my son in his conversion of a previous narrow boat. This was the Venus, a traditionally built oak and elm craft that had seen many years service with the Severn River Authority. The boat had been purchased by this body from the Grand Union Canal Carrying Co., to which she had been originally supplied. She was a motor unit of two prototype wooden pairs, the H class, built by Harland and Wolff in 1934 - 35. Her service with the Severn River Authority at an end, she had lain in the short remaining section of the disused Stroudwater canal, near to its junction with the Gloucester-Sharpness Ship canal at Saul. When purchased by Jeremy she was partially submerged, with her two-cylinder Russell Newberry diesel engine and gearbox under water. Over several years of patient work the engine and gearbox were overhauled and the boat converted, with three cabins, saloon, bathroom, galley and solid fuel central heating and hot water system.

In contrast to Venus, Barrhead is a steel boat, a butty, one of the R or Town class, a numerous type built for the G.U.C.C.C. to exploit the expected increase of trade that it was hoped would result from the modernization of the trunk line. Constructed in 1937, she was registered at Rickmansworth in September of that year. She was sold sometime before January 1, 1948—the date on which the G.U.C.C.C. was nationalised—to a manufacturing business with factories on the River Stort, working for about ten years transporting materials between departments. She had lain, derelict and abandoned, at Bishop's Stortford on the Lee and Stort Navigation before being purchased by Jeremy and Philip in 1969.

Here, they were faced with the problem of finding some economical way of getting her to Gloucester. A commercial boat owner was contacted and he agreed to tow the hull to Braunston on his next run to the Midlands.

In the interest of economy and with the same spirit of resourcefulness which characterized the whole conversion of the boat, Jeremy and his young wife Wendy set out by train one morning to move the boat from Braunston to Worcester. Motive power was to be provided by a 4 h.p. Seagull outboard motor which they took along with them. At Braunston a rough wooden frame was made to drop over the back end to support the motor and with a waterproof sheet under which to sleep, some simple food and a small picnic stove, the hull was laboriously worked through to Diglis

Basin. They lived mostly, I understand, on fish and chips and beer. The weather was rainy and cold and the going painfully slow, an average of something under 1 m.p.h. The little Seagull looked ridiculous on the back of the 70 ft. long butty and its fuel tank needed almost continuous refilling. The bare hull sat like an empty tin can on the water and, with so little power, was affected greatly by the slightest breeze. Any little headwind reduced progress to a snail's pace—sometimes they even went backwards ! It is no wonder that the journey took over seven days.

As the passage from Worcester to Gloucester in the current of the Severn could not be contemplated with the Seagull, arrangements were made with a friend to tow the boat with his ex R.A.F. rescue launch. The owner of the launch had a reputation for being more than a trifle mad and the journey down-stream behind the 120 h.p. craft turned out to be a most hair-raising experience as, with so little of the butty in the water, she was almost uncontrollable. Approaching Gloucester lock with the current—after what must have been the fastest ever run down-river—the tow over-ran the launch, causing them to tangle and almost go down the weir channel out of control.

That the launch owner was, to say the least of it, adventurous, was proved a month later when he signified his intention of making the river passage from Sharpness round the Loop to Gloucester, a trip fraught with the utmost danger for anyone not fully conversant with the fierce tides and shifting sandbanks. To avert what he thought might be a tragedy, another friend who lives on the river and who is familiar with its behaviour thought he had better go along as pilot. There were many factors to be taken into consideration, speed of the boat, predicted height of the tide, speed of the current and the time of departure from Sharpness among other things. Accurate calculations were necessary in order to bring the vessel to Gloucester at the exact time when there would be enough water in the channel to take her over the weir bar, but not so much as would impede her passage under the railway bridge. The margin of error here is small as there is neither time nor space to stooge or manoeuvre between the two. The Gloucester-Sharpness canal was constructed to by-pass this treacherous stretch of the Severn and craft do not normally enter the river again till the lock, which is above the weir. It can be reported that the pilot got all his sums right and that the launch safely ran the gauntlet into the safe water above the railway bridge.

Barrhead in course of conversion, Gloucester Docks.

Barrhead in course of conversion, Gloucester Docks.

There was however a tragic sequel, for a few months later the owner of the boat was found gassed in the cabin of his craft, the reason probably a fault in the cooker installation, but a mystery that was not resolved at the subsequent inquest.

Initial work on the hull of Barrhead was some preliminary scraping and cleaning before it was bow-hauled to the little dry-dock at Hempstead, about a mile out of the city on the ship-canal. A suitable ex-admiralty stern shaft and tube had already been procured and with the required aperture cut in the hull this was welded in position, together with a rudder post and bracket, a heavy skeg and protection plates for the propellor. Outlet plates and sea-cocks for sink, wash-basin and bath and engine cooling were then fitted. Stiffening plates for the propellor shaft brackets and guard plates were also cut and welded in place. The outside of the hull was then scraped and cleaned and coated with several applications of tar, well laced with a suitable drying agent. It was then moved back into the Victoria Basin for completion.

Floor supports of ordinary timber were then fixed over the 4 in. Tee section keelson, leaving just room for the 4 in. concrete blocks which form the ballast. The floor itself, of ¾ in. chipboard, was fitted in sections, unfixed, to facilitate inspection of the hull bottom.

The conversion from butty to motor-boat meant that an engine housing had to be provided and here the converters were blessed with a large share of good fortune. It was learned that British Waterways Board in the area was replacing the engine housings of its working narrow boats with standard fibre glass productions. An urgent and immediate investigation disclosed that a steel housing had just been cut from the narrow boat Pegasus—a K type motor built in 1935 for the G.U.C.C.C.—and that this valuable discard was at that moment on a large heap, awaiting collection by the scrap merchant. A hasty rescue operation was mounted with Land Rover and trailer. The housing was retrieved without too much difficulty and later introduced to the butty at the basin. With the Land Rover in four-wheel drive and the aid of a steel cable over a pulley—which unfortunately could not be mounted overhead—the lucky aquisition was somehow manoeuvred into position on the hull and arc-welded in place.

The question of interior lay-out had already been under discussion and with the experience of living aboard Venus to go upon, it had been decided that a more spacious saloon and a rather bigger galley would make for more comfortable conditions.

Much thought had also been given to the construction of the superstructure. Cement and sand mixture upon steel reinforcing had been considered but this idea was discarded as it was thought that such large flat areas would be unable to dissipate stresses and strain without cracking. Fibreglass laid upon T and G timber, plywood and blockboard were also contemplated, but these methods were turned down as it was thought that they would lack rigidity and that any lateral flexing of the boat would cause cracks and consequent rainwater leaks. It was decided finally to build the superstructure with $\frac{3}{4}$ in. chipboard bolted to 3 in. × 3 in. angle steel frames. These latter were made with a 'tumble home' angle to match that of the engine housing and braced with gusset plates welded into the top corners. The roof span was cambered slightly for appearance after checking that the chipboard would take this curve without difficulty. The frames, spaced 3 ft. 6 ins. apart, were then bolted and welded to the sides of the hull. The box section formed by the frames and hull and the lateral strength of the chipboard provide great rigidity throughout the length of the boat.

The chipboard was first treated with one coat of sealing resin, this was followed by another coat with a covering of fibreglass mat. Then followed another application of resin with a covering of film and finally a finishing coat of resin containing the green dye to conform to the colour scheme which had been decided upon.

In practice the construction has proved entirely satisfactory. There have sometimes been as many as a dozen people at a time on the roof and though the boat has been well used—grounding hard amidships and stemming up on solid obstacles on many occasions—no fault whatever has shown itself.

As it was intended that the boat should be used at all seasons, adequate light has been arranged with a large part of the side area taken up by windows. As commercially made units of this size and number would cost a great deal of money, the hopper type were decided upon as these could be made quite inexpensively on the spot.

By this time the means of providing an engine and gearbox had been given some serious thought. As the cost of marine units, even secondhand, was considered to be out of the question, some other way of procuring suitable power had to be found. The problem appeared to be solved one day when Philip—a veterinary surgeon—in the course of his duties, noticed a badly smashed-up Ford truck in the corner of a farmyard. The vehicle had only covered a very moderate mileage and after some ‘ cattle-market haggling ’ with the farmer, a bargain price was agreed upon for the whole truck. This was then dismantled and the chassis cut off at the required length. With supporting brackets welded to the hull, the shortened chassis section was then bolted into the boat and the engine installed on its original bearers. This was then coupled to a Parsons marine gearbox—obtained for a song—also mounted on the chassis section. The truck tail shaft, shortened to suit, but with its own universal joints, was then fitted between this and the propellor shaft of the boat.

A handsome bronze water pump that had already seen some service on an industrial machine was fitted to the engine in place of the brake exhauster unit. This circulates canal and river water round a closed engine cooling circuit formed with a brass header-tank—picked up from a scrap yard—and suitable copper piping.

The three interconnected fuel tanks once did duty as oil storage tanks on a garage forecourt. Mounted high at the back end of the engine room they feed the engine by gravity and have a combined capacity of 90 gallons.

The doors at each end of the living section are of Utile, with glass panels in the forward ones, and were professionally made. The whole of the inside is insulated with 1″ thick fibreglass and, with the exception of the bathroom which is covered with hardboard, is lined with varnished pine matchboarding. Saloon and cabin furnishings, galley fittings, airing cupboard (housing the hot water tank) and bunks were constructed on the boat. The bathroom has a short bath, a washbasin—both ex-building alterations—and a space for the chemical closet. Plans are in hand to replace this with a wash-down model, in which case a storage tank will be installed with a diaphragm pump for emptying purposes.

At this stage of the work almost all of the converters' spare time was being devoted to the project, a dedication which appears common to all fanatics who, in the words of dear old A. P. Herbert, spend their leisure days ‘ messing about in boats.’

My mind is taken back some fifteen years to a mooring on a canal arm where a score of boats were being maintained and converted. The enthusiast on the next mooring owned a small 15ft. cabin cruiser. He lived in London and would arrive every holiday time with some new equipment or fitting that he had purchased or prefabricated in the interim. These innovations would be installed with great ceremony and with many assurances as to their safety value when eventually he would take his boat into the river and down to the estuary. His wife in the background would raise her eyes from her knitting and, with a tolerant smile on her face, slowly move her head from side to side. She knew, without any doubt whatever, that he would never take the boat from the mooring and in fact, for as long as we were there he never did.

One holiday time he arrived with a new sea toilet and this, for ease of connection was mounted as near as possible to the sea-cock outlet. To connect it he had brought a length of $2\frac{1}{2}$ in. bore, semi-rigid transparent plastic tube. As, due to the acuteness of the bend, it was impossible to make a short connecting link, the whole length had to be employed. It must have been an absolutely fantastic experience to sit and work the pump handle and watch the contents of the loo describe a graceful arc before one's eyes before disappearing over the left shoulder and out of the sea-cock.

Barrhead has a radiator in the bathroom and one in each of the cabins. Hot water for these and the galley is provided by a solid fuel boiler of modern design, again secondhand. In the milder weather this provides ample heat and hot water from the plentiful supply of dead wood always to be found around the towing paths of the canals. In the winter a stock of anthracite is carried when the boiler works round the clock.

Jeremy and Philip were somewhat disappointed and they hesitated for some time before paying full prices for a new copper hot water cylinder and bottled gas cooker.

In the forepeak is the 250 gall. fresh water tank, another garage oil storage unit, cleansed and painted inside with synthetic enamel. Water from this is pumped to a header tank, located in the bathroom, by a high-pressure electric motor-car fuel pump, controlled by a float valve. This enables the bathroom and galley units to be fed by gravity.

The size and pitch of the propellor were calculated by standard formula from engine power and speed, size and shape of hull and other factors. In practice the power unit, a Ford 4D, has proved most satisfactory and has never given a moment's trouble. With ample power available, the injection pump throttle stop has been set to give a maximum engine speed of 1400 r.p.m. and this provides a water speed of about 7 m.p.h., well in excess of anything allowed on the canals. This margin of power and speed is very necessary for operating the boat in rivers such as the Severn in winter time, when the freshets from the Welsh Hills increase the force of the stream considerably.

Electrical storage is provided by two 12 volt heavy duty tractor batteries and lighting throughout is by fluorescent tube. A small charging plant is installed in the engine compartment for emergencies but, with the boat in regular use, it has never been found necessary to call upon this.

No alteration whatever was made to the hull proper, but one point is worthy of mention, the wise provision of a 2 in. sill below the doorway opening on to the forward well deck. In some of the fast-filling wide locks, such as those on the Grand Union, there was so much turbulence that water came through the scupper holes and the saloon would have suffered serious flooding without this provision. On the narrow canals where the boat almost filled the chamber, this did not occur.

By the early summer of 1973 the work was nearing completion. A trial run up the Severn proved the behaviour and working of the boat to be most satisfactory, but it was decided to make some small modification to the engine cooling system.

Lastly the exterior painting was completed and this included the usual cabin decorations incorporating a highly imaginative castle among the scrolls and flowers.

With the fuel tanks filled to capacity and all the non-perishable stores aboard, everyone concerned could now look forward to the relaxing and well earned holidays that had been planned.

It was a dull day at the beginning of August and a fine rain was falling when I joined Barrhead in the Victoria Basin of Gloucester Docks.

The aim of these first two weeks of our holiday was to travel the Severn as far as Worcester, transferring to the Worcester and Birmingham canal, then to the Stratford-on-Avon canal, the Grand Union and Oxford canals and finally the upper Thames to Inglesham, just above Lechlade, where the romantic but now defunct Thames and Severn canal made its junction with the capital river. We were sad indeed that this unique waterway, with its 3,187 yds. long tunnel through the Sapperton Hill, together with the now disused Stroudwater, could not be used to make a junction with the

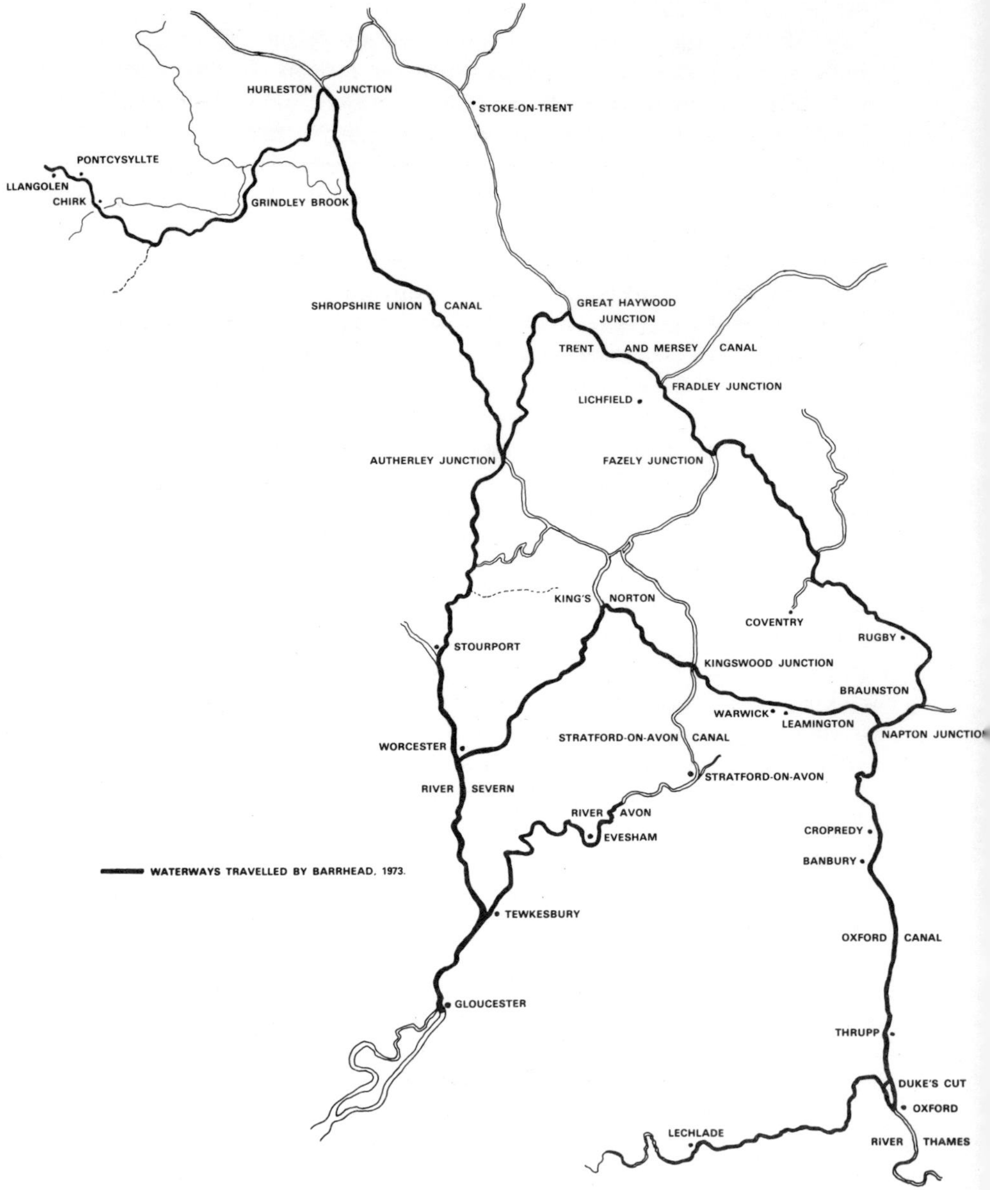

HURLESTON
JUNCTION
STOKE-ON-TRENT
PONTCYSYLLTE
LLANGOLEN
CHIRK
GRINDLEY BROOK
SHROPSHIRE UNION
CANAL
GREAT HAYWOOD
JUNCTION
TRENT
AND MERSEY
CANAL
FRADLEY JUNCTION
LICHFIELD
AUTHERLEY JUNCTION
FAZELY JUNCTION
KING'S
NORTON
COVENTRY
RUGBY
STOURPORT
KINGSWOOD JUNCTION
BRAUNSTON
WARWICK
LEAMINGTON
NAPTON JUNCTION
WORCESTER
STRATFORD-ON-AVON
CANAL
STRATFORD-ON-AVON
RIVER
SEVERN
RIVER
AVON
EVESHAM
CROPREDY
BANBURY
WATERWAYS TRAVELLED BY BARRHEAD, 1973.
TEWKESBURY
OXFORD
CANAL
GLOUCESTER
THRUPP
DUKE'S CUT
OXFORD
LECHLADE
RIVER
THAMES

Gloucester-Sharpness ship canal, when a full round trip could have been accomplished.

The Thames and Severn canal when it was opened in 1783 effected the long dreamed of marriage, first mooted as early as the beginning of the 17th century, between England's two major rivers. The sedate and slow-moving Father Thames, well controlled by its many locks and weirs, was romantically joined to the capricious and unpredictable Sabrina. Though comparatively docile in the dry season and well-behaved within its high banks, the Severn is still largely untamed. Wilful and headstrong in the rainy season, it often surges over its protecting banks to inundate the surrounding countryside.

My son Jeremy and myself, as members of the Inland Waterways Association, are very much concerned with the maintenance and preservation of the canals and their use both for pleasure and commercial purposes. The object of the journey—apart of course from the holiday aspect and the pleasure derived from working the boat—was part of an all-over plan to cover in the course of time as much as possible of the country's canal system.

Although wives and children were coming along and we were taking a few luxuries, including a portable television set to keep the children entertained, I have refrained from calling the venture a cruise. Nautical terms were never used by the canal fraternity or administration and we were endeavouring to make the actual working of the boat and the approach to the run as authentic as possible.

Barrhead lay against the wharf wall in the rectangular arm of the docks, her predominantly yellow, red and green decorations a welcome splash of colour amid drab surroundings. The tall warehouses, their multitude of windows dusty and neglected, stood now mostly empty and silent, sad memorials of the time when the docks bristled with the masts of trows, frigates and other craft loading and discharging their varied merchandise at its wharves. Several large capacity grain barges, brooded over by the ghostly buildings, silently waited for their next call into service. In a corner of the arm a derelict and lifeless steam tug patiently awaited her inevitable fate at the hands of the breakers.

My dark reflections on the scene were quickly lightened by the excited chatter of children as Jeremy and Philip arrived with their families. We were also joined by Norman, a friend and canal enthusiast, who would take turns in the working of the boat. Philip,

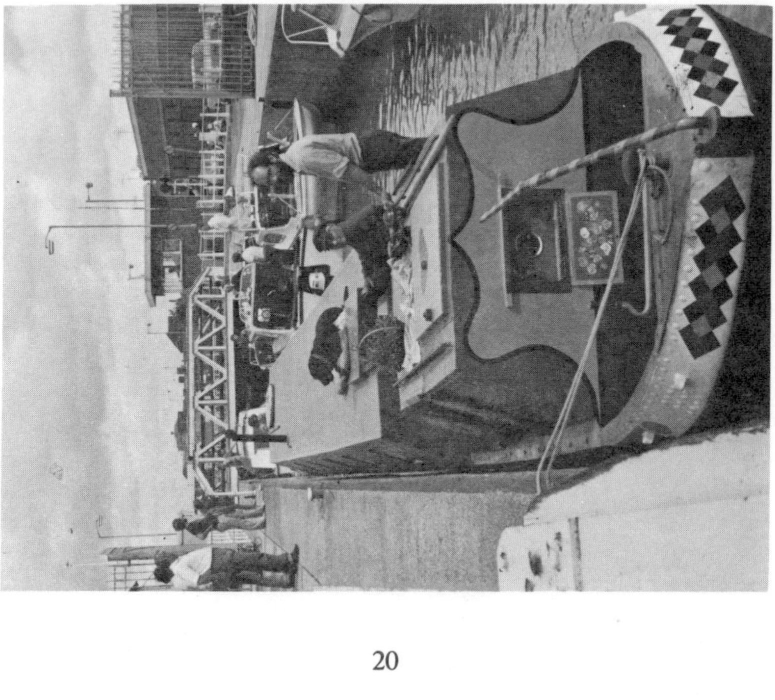

Locking into the Severn. Gloucester Docks.

Champagne from plastic cups. Jeremy and Philip.

an avid sportsman with the gun, had brought his large black retriever Sweep, who was to greatly improve his swimming speed and endurance before the holiday was over.

With personal belongings stored and four young children safely life-jacketed and aboard, the engine was started and we made our way round the docks to the lock. It was due to open at 11.0 a.m. Here we joined several small cruisers which were also going up-stream and in due course of time were lowered a few feet to the level of the river. This was almost at its lowest and ebbing strongly.

The large lock, 150 ft. long and 22 ft. wide, is capable of taking the largest vessel that could ever conceivably use the river above this point. The pleasure craft preceded us like a family of ducks as we followed them through the gates into the river.

The stream was muddy, a product of the recent rains, and at three-quarter engine speed, against the current, we estimated that we were making about 6 m.p.h. over the ground. The Upper Parting, where the river divides to make its excursion round Alney Island, was passed on our lefthand while we made steady progress against the now decreasing current. Coal House Inn, once a staging point for trows and other sailing barges using the river was passed with great reluctance by the crew as, in keeping with tradition, they usually made a stop here.

In Wainlode Pool—just below Norton—we arrived at the point where the Bristol Channel tides become spent and cease to reverse the flow of the stream. It is here, on the bend before Haw Bridge, that the river is joined by the disused Coombe Hill canal, a broad 2¾ mile long, almost straight waterway with only two locks at its junction with the Severn. In its short and chequered career it served the important spa of Cheltenham, with the great disadvantage that, with the absence of any further locks, it was obliged to terminate at the foot of Coombe Hill, some miles short of the town. Also here, a little down-stream from the canal locks, the river is joined by the diminutive Chelt Brook, from which the town takes its name.

Further on at Deerhurst there is a mooring and within very short walking distance lies the ancient Odda's Chapel. The Saxon church of the place, dated 1056, is also near at hand. Both places are well worth a visit, but in this instance we did not stop as we had our sights on things further afield.

Sweep, the retriever, not yet in possession of his 'sea legs', moved around with a singular lack of confidence, his belly no more

Winter. Worcester—Birmingham Canal.

The Avon in flood and a casualty.

than a few inches from the shiny, cambered roof top of the saloon. He finally decided that the Severn scenery could be viewed with more equanimity from the refuge of a lifebelt, of which he took almost permanent possession till the canals were reached.

The Upper Lode lock, large and impressive, looked very well maintained and efficient as we were passed through in company with several smaller vessels. All of the latter turned up the Avon while we kept to the main stream.

A few weeks previously Jeremy and Philip had taken Barrhead up the Avon on a trial run, with the fond hope that the industrious members of the Upper Avon Navigation Trust, now working on the last obstacle, might have completed their task. It would have been thrilling indeed had they been able to get through to the southern section of the Stratford canal, but it was not to be. The boat did however make a little history on that occasion, for an old river man came forward with the information that she had been the first full length narrow boat since 1880 to get so high up this long neglected route to the Midlands. Great credit is due to the resourceful volunteers whose unstinting efforts, with the skilled assistance of the Royal Engineers, have already made this possible.

The Severn is not a beautiful river and there is little of real interest upon which to comment, but some light relief was afforded by the antics of a small cruiser which we met just below Upton-on-Severn. This had obviously just been hired and the man at the helm, still very nervous and unsure of his charge, appeared to take fright as we neared one another. He zig-zagged about in our path in a most disconcerting manner and we were under some apprehension as it was impossible to predict on which side he would ultimately pass. He apparently did not know himself. We were left in no doubt when he steered directly across the stream and plunged his bows into the vegetation on the left bank. There were some frantic efforts with the reverse gear and rudder before he managed to extricate himself. Following a few more gyrations he suddenly turned hard across the river in front of us to charge the opposite bank. The poor man and his family looked most embarrassed and abashed as we came abreast. The pertinent advice offered by one of the crew to "Try putting the handbrake on" was intended to be humorous, but seemed a little cruel in the circumstances.

Once through Diglis lock on the river we turned almost immediately into the first of the two locks which lifted Barrhead a total of 18 ft. to the level of the basin. This also makes a common level with the first pound on the Worcester-Birmingham canal.

With no assurance as to how long our proposed run to Inglesham would take, everyone was anxious to make as much progress as possible in the early stages, so no stop was made at Worcester. We passed under several bridges carrying the busy city traffic over the canal and climbed the locks to the suburbs.

Number four lock, Blockhouse, is, as my son found to his cost, the narrowest on the Worcester-Birmingham line, indeed the narrowest in his experience. It was on a previous passage with Venus, some five years earlier, that he became well and truly imprisoned in its chamber. At the time of the jamming incident she was on her first trip after conversion. With age the walls of a lock chamber are always prone to bulge inwards a little and when Venus was put into Blockhouse it was found that she would not go in far enough to enable the bottom gates to be closed. Jeremy, who is never one to be discouraged by such a situation as this, reversed out of the chamber and came smartly back in under a fair amount of power. Venus went in a little further but stuck hard and fast, her back end and rudder still fouling the bottom gates. Fortunately they were carrying some 15 cwt. differential chain-lifting blocks. Equipment such as this is very useful when exploring some of the more neglected and less used canals. The blocks were secured to a telegraph pole on the towpath and a strong rope passed round the boat. Despite all the strain which they could exert with this she still refused to budge. This effort was then supplemented by quick flashes of water through the top gates. Two of the crew would quickly wind up the paddles and it was found that the ensuing rush of water, in conjunction with the strain on the rope, would move the boat about an inch. This sequence was kept up for hours till the level in the lower pound rose so much that the towpath became flooded. They did not know, but the water going over the gates of the locks lower down was causing flooding in the city. The first intimation of trouble was the appearance of a canal employee cycling hard up the towpath, shouting and waving his arms as he came. Unfortunately this zealous servant of the waterway was so intent on attracting the attention of the narrow boat's crew that he failed to observe the rope stretched across the towpath, submerged in his precious water. The lower extension of his front mudguard caught in this and he was precipitated over the handlebars, to land

Venus. Staffs. and Worcester Canal.

Sawing wire from propellor of Venus.

on his hands and knees in about 6 in. of water. He addressed the crew forcibly from a kneeling position and it was very obvious from his language that he was not saying his prayers.

" W'ot the 'ell d'ya think you be up to, you'll 'ave 'alf the bloody city flooded if ya' don't stop."

Picking up his bicycle he came up to them, swearing about his wet clothes. He became a little more reasonable as the difficulty was explained. Eventually some sort of peace was arrived at with the promise of only very sparing use of further water.

By early evening the boat was freed, but it had taken a whole day of very hard work to accomplish.

The inability to negotiate the lock brought about a complete change of plan which necessitated a return to the Severn and a run up-stream to Stourport, where Venus was taken on to the Staffs and Worcester canal.

Over the years the oak sides of Venus had expanded a little, but Barrhead does not exceed the standard 7 ft. beam, so no difficulty was experienced in Blockhouse lock in this instance.

At Blackpole everyone agreed to call it a day and we tied up for the night—opposite a pub of course—in true canal fashion.

Our start in the morning soon brought trouble, one of the many occasions when the screw picked up rubbish from the canal bottom. The canals, particularly where they pass through cities and towns and other built-up areas appear to be the favourite dumping place for oil drums, old bicycles, car tyres and a multitude of other unwanted items.

A few years ago a friend on a journey through another Midlands canal rounded a bend just in time to see a piano slowly sinking out of sight and a small van driving away from the bridge from which the unwanted instrument had just been thrown.

In our case it was nothing so romantic, a mere agricultural plastic sack, a bicycle tyre, a scarf and the fabric and ribs of a broken umbrella which had wound themselves tightly round the screw and its shaft. These were removed with some difficulty by boathooks and the sharp use of reverse gear.

The worst case that I know of was that experienced by my son when the propellor of his narrow boat Venus picked up the steel skeleton of a box spring mattress in Debdale lock on the Staffs and Worcester canal—a double bed size at that too. The tempered steel wire from which this was constructed wound itself inextricably round the screw, its shaft and the rudder post. The first inkling of trouble was a sickening thud as the diesel engine was brought to an abrupt stop. On examination it was discovered that the sudden increase in torque exerted by the energy stored in its heavy flywheel had distorted the propellor shaft.

This was a saddening blow just at the beginning of a holiday as it subsequently caused vibration and excessive wear in the bearing and gland but it did not prevent the crew from completing the tour that had been planned.

An investigation overside in bathing trunks disclosed that there was no hope whatever of unwinding the mattress. Over a pint at the nearby inn it was learned that the owner of a local timber yard possessed a mobile crane. The man was contacted and persuaded to help and in due course the machine arrived on the scene. By using a heavy chain which was passed under her bottom, the crane was able to lift the back end of the boat a couple of feet to bring the obstruction nearer the surface. Standing in the canal the crew set about what seemed an almost impossible task. It took about six hours of hard work with wire cutters and hacksaws to cut through the hundreds of tempered steel strands and break it free.

A valuable lesson was learnt that day in Debdale lock, for Barrhead has two large $\frac{1}{2}$ in. thick semi-circular guard plates, welded one above and one below the screw and a disaster such as this is unlikely to happen again.

There is a great temptation to moralise here, but the dumping of unwanted rubbish is a national problem, indeed a world problem, and not an evil confined solely to waterways.

Rain was falling steadily as we left Blackpole and prepared to ascend the remainder of the 58 locks, all packed into 16 miles, which lift the canal from Worcester to the summit of the Lickey Hills. This series, terminating in the Tardebigge flight of 30 closely spaced locks, is the longest in the country, with a total rise of 425 ft.

The 236 yds. long Dunhampstead tunnel in this section, our first excursion underground on this trip, proved the fitting of twin headlamps to have been well worthwhile as these could be trimmed to illuminate both sides of the working.

In the Stoke section it was interesting to see the various arms branching away to serve the salt workings around Stoke Prior.

It is sad to see any disused waterway and we experienced the usual feelings of nostalgia as we peered into the desolate junction of the

Droitwich canal, engineered by Brindley and used mostly for the salt trade. This short waterway has since that time been the scene of much industry by a large band of enthusiastic volunteers, aided by some mechanical equipment, and there are very real hopes that the reopening of this canal may not be too long delayed.

Our clothes were now thoroughly wet but we were making good time despite the weather. The crew, young and energetic, tackled and operated each lock with true professionalism. The boat was lined up in good time and driven confidently through the open gates with great aplomb by the steerer, though there were only a few inches to spare. The others went ahead to set the gates and paddles. My job only consisted of the closing of one bottom gate, but it was hard work indeed keeping up with them as the actual time of each transit was little more than five minutes. The gates on the Worcester -Birmingham are light and easy to handle and the paddle gear is free-running and generally in good fettle. The chambers are also very quick in filling.

At about 9 p.m., in the rain-swept dusk, we negotiated the last few locks which curved away round the hillside and passed the pumping station below the summit. This lifts water from the extensive feeder reservoir which could be seen away to the right to supplement the store in the long top pound, which includes the Birmingham levels and the Stratford canal to Lapworth. The final lift to the summit here is effected by the deepest narrow lock in the country, all of 14 ft.

Much to the disgust of a very wet and bedraggled crew, a search of the dismal surroundings of the Tardebigge maintenance yard failed to disclose the existence of a tavern to lighten the gloom. After topping up our 250 gall. water tank we tied up to a British Waterways working narrow boat and everyone turned in. The children had been fast asleep for some time.

The next morning was fine and almost immediately after leaving the yard behind we entered the 580 yds long Tardebigge tunnel. This is one of several tunnels and cuttings on this level where, after the concentrated 30 lock climb up to the summit, the engineer appeared resolved at all costs to avoid further lifts. With the Birmingham Level Navigations and the stretch of the Stratford-on-Avon canal to the top lock at Lapworth mentioned earlier, there is a total of almost 50 miles of waterway without a lock, and this at 450 ft. above sea level. It was noticed in this section that much piling and dredging is badly needed.

Somewhere in the black depths of the 2,726 yds long Wast Hill tunnel we passed from Worcestershire into Warwickshire.

At King's Norton, on the outskirts of Birmingham, we forsook the route which led on into the city and turned right to squeeze Barrhead through the narrow lock into the Stratford canal. This lock, with its quaint guillotine gate, is now permanently open.

The country about us was level but not uninteresting and we had ahead of us a run to Lapworth without a lock. Despite this, the passage of the Stratford canal proved to be second only in difficulty to our journeyings on the Llangollen canal, of which more later.

Barrhead draws about 2 ft. 6 ins. and even on the Worcester-Birmingham line—away from the middle—we often found ourselves on the mud, particularly on the sharper bends. Here however, on the Stratford, we were ploughing hard through the mud in its centre for most of the way to Lapworth. For nearly all of this distance we estimated that we were making only 1 m.p.h. The route is much used by pleasure craft, the great majority of them of shallow draught, and these vessels set up more wash than the deeper draught boats. Many of the hirers exceed the limit of 4 m.p.h. fixed by British Waterways and prominently displayed on their notice boards. It must however be said in mitigation that this is probably due to bad judgement rather than a disregard for the rules. In the few places where the banks are piled there is more water, but where the sides are unprotected, the wash from passing boats is gradually bringing down more and more material into the middle. With comparatively few deeper draught boats going through, the general depth of the canal is steadily becoming more restricted.

With their limited funds there is no doubt that British Waterways are doing all that they are able. Everyone knows that the answer to the foregoing problem is more and more dredging and piling. On this canal and in places on the Grand Union and Oxford lines, trees and vegetation have encroached on the waterway, sometimes taking up as much as half its width. It is felt that the clearing of such overgrowth is maintenance work which would not absorb large labour forces and not entail a huge expense. If adequate financial aid were forthcoming there is no reason why our canals and their towpaths could not be kept as clear and tidy as are our roads, the best in the world, we like to think.

Near Shirley we met two hotel boats—with a short towline

between them—on a bend where fortunately there was just enough water for all of us. These were excellent conversions, professionally constructed on a traditionally built motor boat and butty. They were well handled too. The motor boat, still in her original livery, retained the stove pipe, water carrier and dipper, and the brass embellishments of these and the tiller handle sparkled in the morning sunshine. From the roof of the engine compartment rose an authentic exhaust pipe and out of this issued the lusty thump—thump—thump of her single-cylinder Bolinder diesel engine, the original no doubt. These marvellous old bits of machinery scorned such sissy things as starting motors and the starting of one from cold on a frosty morning, in the confined space of the engine compartment, was not a job for weaklings. The starting device was a steel rod which one pulled out from the rim of the flywheel against the pressure of a spring. The whole thing retracted quickly into the solid wheel when it was released. Much knack was required and if the peak of human effort on the starting rod was not timed to coincide with the point where the large diameter piston came on compression, it could fire back, whereupon one could be hurled against the side of the engine housing as though kicked by a more than usually bad-tempered mule.

I can recall some bitter experiences when starting a large single-cylinder four-stroke agricultural diesel engine. The technique was to rotate this by hand in a forward direction till the piston bounced off compression, then moving quickly to the opposing side of the flywheel to pull on the rim and gain momentum backwards, finally jumping onto a spoke as the piston again came on compression. If all was well the engine would fire forward and proceed to run on its best behaviour. Needless to say it was very necessary to get one's feet clear of the flywheel at the crucial moment. On one or two occasions, perhaps due to over-enthusiasm in jumping on the flywheel spokes, it had gone right over compression and fired back viciously, proceeding to run at a fair speed in counter rotation. This meant that the inlet valve—not the exhaust valve—opened following the firing stroke. It was a pretty frightening experience in the confined space, fumbling around in the dimness and with smarting eyes to locate the fuel stop, while the barking monster shot long flames and belched blue diesel vapour out of the air intake.

On this occasion however the Bolinder in the hotel boat was behaving perfectly and running steadily.

The steerer of the butty was a most attractive female in blue jeans and a red blouse. As we came abreast she smiled sweetly and leant far out in our direction to push the tiller to its limit and negotiate the bend. The craft made a brave sight in the sunshine and there was unqualified approval that they were a " lovely pair ", inspiring the comment from one of the closely observant males that " The boats were pretty good too."

Our hard slog through the Upper Stratford canal at length brought us to the head of the Lapworth flight of locks, many of them very close together. Whenever locks were fairly closely spaced the opportunity was taken to give the children some exercise. They are of varying ages, Frances six, Michael four, Richard three and little Helen still short of her second birthday. Mostly they had to amuse themselves on the boat and the saloon table and floor were usually littered with miniature motor vehicles, drawing paper, crayons and the like. On the towpath they became completely uninhibited and ran around like a litter of lively puppies, pulling on the lock arms and generally prying into everything. After a few days of keeping them under close observation all the grown-ups had developed swivelling necks like owls.

After the descent of the Lapworth flight we locked through the short link at Kingswood to join the Grand Union. Here we were on a wide, deep canal, with an unrestricted run to the Hatton locks. The boat ran freely with plenty of water under her bottom and after our ditch crawling on the Stratford we felt as though we were on a motorway.

Barrhead was now in home water. Doubtless she had passed this way many times breasted up to her motor boat on the coal run from the Staffordshire pits. As mentioned earlier she was one of many of her class, all named after towns in the British Isles.

The Grand Union mostly is a well preserved waterway, only in places where there is no bank protection are the silt and reeds invading the thoroughfare. In a few other places large trees cause some hindrance where they hang low over the water. The concrete piling is excellent and we noted the details cast into it; generally these indicated that they were driven 5 ft. 6 ins. to 6 ft. 6 ins. below water line and dredged to 3 ft. 6 ins.

At the Hatton locks it was a change to operate the smoothly working worm drive paddle gear. The old locks beside the new are interesting relics from pre-modernization days. The tower of St.

Barrhead and Camping boat.
Cape of Good Hope Inn, Grand Union Canal.

New Bridge and Maybush Inn, River Thames.

Mary's church, Warwick, could be seen below us as we came down the flight.

Here it was decided to moor for the night, near to the Cape of Good Hope inn, though we could not get nearer than 3 ft. to the wharf because of the shallow water. This is a popular place and a dozen or so hire boats and privately owned craft were moored along the tow path. Later another holiday craft, one of a fleet of camping boats, moved in and tied up outside us for the night. These are authentic narrow boats, well maintained and still very much in their original condition. What was the cargo space is covered by a stout, very well made canvas sheet, like a tent, supported by the original foot planks on their cratches and stands. As has been said, these boats are very much as they were in their working days. We were able to examine with interest the engine and gearbox and admire the brass embellishments on the stove chimney, the water can and dipper and the tiller handle. The Ram's Head and other rope work were newly pipe-clayed and altogether she made a lovely sleeping companion.

The next morning we passed under many bridges on the 'Five Mile Level' and skirting Leamington started to climb again at Radford Bottom lock.

At the Fosse locks we dumped our rubbish. British Waterways are to be commended for the well spaced and well appointed sewage and waste disposal stations. In one or two places we found the storage capacity strained to overflowing, but this was the height of the season and perhaps the collectors were on holiday.

About mid-day we made our next stop at the Blue Lias Inn, an attractive place situated in the gentle rise covered by the Stockton locks. The inn was well known to some of the crew from past experience. Mine host had spared no effort to be helpful when the engine of Venus had broken an exhaust valve on a previous trip. It was decided to stay here till the morning as the children were in need of change and exercise.

After breakfast it was but a short run to Napton Junction where we left the wide waterway and turned on to the narrow, truly rural Oxford canal. A pleasant mile or so through farming country and we were at the Napton locks, eight of them, which step up to the disused branch known as the Old Engine House Arm. Here the canal makes a wide sweep round Napton Hill and we were given a panoramic view of its famous stone-built windmill on the skyline.

We regret to say that the gaunt buildings of the brickworks were not such a pleasant sight.

From here on one gains the impression that this waterway, one of the oldest in the country, assumes a completely different character. It would seem that Brindley, who was its engineer, after his flurry of locks at Napton was determined to take every advantage of the undulating terrain and avoid at all costs any cuttings or locks. An incredibly tortuous route is traced as the canal winds round every little depression and skirts each hump of rising ground, truly a contour canal. These deviations only served to enhance our enjoyment, for the countryside around was the most peaceful and charming that we had found. There was field after field of ripening corn, in some of which the combine harvesters were already at work. On this remote section no built up area is encountered till Banbury and the waterway only touches a few isolated villages. Some piling of the banks was being undertaken here but the tow-paths are densely overgrown for long stretches.

In country such as this, where the body can relax and the mind be mended, a holiday on the canals can be fully appreciated. The whole tempo of life is perforce slowed down to 4 m.p.h. and that arch villain of our environment, the motor car, seems part of another world.

This canal was, in its early days, the great coal route from the Midlands to Oxford and London, but its picturesque twisting course contributed largely to its undoing when the wider, more direct Grand Trunk came into being.

The river Cherwell introduces itself near Cropredy lock and remains a close travelling companion till they both join the Thames at Oxford. Indeed they were wedded in full consummation for a short distance between the weirs near Shipton, before changing sides in their progress down the shallow Cherwell valley.

Here, Sweep the retriever found the most enjoyable part of his holiday, swimming behind us but never quite able to keep up, then taking to the fields as we disappeared from view. He also found time to chase the moorhens and duck from their retreats at the water's edge, but his only success was a mouthful of feathers from one of the latter.

The locks on the Oxford canal were designed to take boats of 70 ft. and no longer and we found that there was very little to spare. In descents it was necessary to keep our stem hard against the mitre posts of the bottom gates with the engine idling in gear, to prevent the rudder from settling on the sill of the top gates as the chamber emptied.

In many places on this canal the banks are protected with what appear to be the original sidewalls, rough-dressed stonework laid with mortar. No doubt this was adequate when the passing traffic was horse-drawn but the wash from powered craft has now brought out much of the bonding material and many of them are falling down.

Banbury, with its famous cross of nursery memory, does not present its best face to travellers on the canal and we were not inspired to make a stop here.

Our mooring for the night was near King's Sutton, just over the county boundary in Northants. The village itself is not easy to reach from the canal as the nearest bridge over the Cherwell is some few miles distant. The nearby disused railway bridge however does cross, and following a jaunt across several fields in semi-darkness, with the church spire as a landmark, the village was eventually reached and thirsts duly assuaged. The place boasted four good inns, all of which received a visit, the drinking rate being regulated accordingly. At the last of these a country hop was being held, with an extension to twelve thirty. With a natural reluctance to leave the convivial atmosphere the crew members were faced with one and a half hours more drinking time than they had bargained for. Perhaps the least said about the return across the fields in the darkness the better and we will draw a veil across the plight of the roisterer who fell flat on to his back from the handrails of the railway bridge before rolling into the canal. Those revellers who stayed in their bunks in the morning and refused breakfast—a most unusual occurrence—shall also remain anonymous.

The next morning a shopping expedition in the light of day proved the village to be a most charming place, quite unspoiled and with no through traffic to ruin its peace and quietness.

Our next stop was at Thrupp, boasting a British Waterways maintenance yard, where we tied up near a long line of canal cottages still very much in their original condition.

Here we were joined by my wife, making our total now eleven. I was able to answer quite truthfully in the affirmative when asked by my grandaughter Frances, " Are you happy now your wife is here ? "

In this reach known as Thrupp Wide many craft are moored,

including several narrow boat conversions and one or two hulls.

The next morning, still in brilliant sunshine we continued our travels. At Kidlington Green we caught up with a pair of hotel boats just preparing to enter the lock and we waited behind while these were put through in turn. At the tail of the lock in the lower pound a commercial narrow boat and butty that had just arrived, also waited. Although we were there before them we were glad to let them take advantage of the empty chamber to put their boats through. The steerer and his wife on the butty were obviously chafed by the delay and they made no attempt to disguise their feelings. Their rude remarks, directed at all and sundry, concerned the use of the canal by holiday boats and pleasure seekers. This attitude by commercial users of the waterways—which we hope and trust is not universal—is quite unjustified as, without the long campaign waged by the I.W.A. and the efforts and practical work of the many volunteer preservation bodies, very few of the thoroughfares would still be navigable.

Immediately following Duke's lock there is a short level cut of only 250 yds, by-passing Oxford and connecting with the Thames. We did not take advantage of this on the outward journey as we were keen to explore the whole canal and go through the city.

The first part of this section runs through the very pleasant Duke's Meadows, with beautifully kept university playing fields on either side. As we got into the city proper we found very little depth of water. It was obvious that no vessel of moderate draught had been along for some time. With the engine at half throttle we literally rode along the mud at a snail's pace and were enabled to make a very close inspection of the back gardens of the houses.

Once through Isis lock we were required to turn back acutely right-handed to pass under the railway swing bridge. On Saturdays and Sundays this is kept open, but at other times there may be delays while traffic or shunting is cleared.

On the spacious waters of the Thames we felt as though we were in the open sea after our ditch crawl through the city. Barrhead, with plenty of water under her, ran as though on ball-bearings. Going up-river we moored for the night in the reach below Godstow lock, within easy walking distance of the Trout Inn.

In the morning we returned down-stream to Osney lock where we were required to submit to a check by a Thames Conservancy Inspector. This official made a careful examination and decided that we just came within the requirements. He was able to issue a registration certificate and licence and we were free to go. We were availing ourselves of one of the short-term licences which are issued to vessels visiting the river from other waters and the fee seemed most reasonable. The regulations, with new specifications issued in 1972, are covered in detail in a booklet called 'Launch Digest', supplied free by the Conservators. All craft on the Thames, irrespective of those carrying goods or used solely as tugs, are designated as launches. A limited speed of 8 m.p.h. is imposed, with sound advice to slow to 2 m.p.h. under certain conditions, such as passing a sculler. Rules for safety are set out in detail in the booklet including stringent precautions to prevent pollution of the river.

It is possible that a private boat owner contemplating a visit to the Thames from the canal system may be dismayed by the formidable list of requirements to cover safety. Much thought has obviously been given to these matters and strict enforcement of the regulations can only be for the benefit of everyone concerned.

It was mid-day before we were cleared and licenced and ready to continue on our way. The passage of the manned locks, very smart in the sunshine and ablaze with colourful flowers, seemed a far cry from our intensive efforts in the climb up the Lickey Hills to Tardebigge in the pouring rain.

We were now sharing locks with a lot of pleasure craft, most of them hired. There was also a sprinkling of lush, expensive looking private cruisers whose owners viewed our bulk and scored black sides with nervous suspicion. The crews, anxious to preserve their glistening paint, made haste to put out a surfeit of impeccable white fenders and, taking up defensive positions, brandished highly-varnished, chromium-ended boathooks menacingly in our direction.

There are plenty of good inns with suitable mooring places on the river and frequent stops were made. We now knew that we had ample time to reach Inglesham and also to work the boat back to a convenient place on the Oxford canal. Here it was proposed to leave her for a few weeks pending the return of some of the crew. As soon as this was possible she would be taken north and on to the Welsh canal before returning to Gloucester.

At the inn stops the children were usually provided with soft drinks and crisps and allowed to run around the lawns. Helen, the youngest, still three months short of her second birthday, who apparently knows everything and seems equally capable of putting her knowledge into words, anticipated these stops with as much relish as the thirsty crew members. On more than one occasion, when the engine revolutions had been reduced for some reason, a little voice had been heard to say, " Are we stopping at a pub, Mummy ? "

One overnight stop was made near New Bridge where there are two good inns, the Rose Revived on the Oxfordshire side of the river and the May Bush on the Berkshire bank. It is here that the most beautiful of all the Cotswold rivers joins the Thames. The clear and sparkling Windrush, after its leisurely journey down from North Gloucestershire, flows into the capital river under this lovely old bridge. The name New Bridge is a misnomer, for the habitues of the May Bush Inn—strongly partisan—claim that it is the oldest bridge crossing the Thames this side of London. A gently-cambered, gracefully built structure in honey coloured stone, its six arches span the confluence of the two rivers. It is much used now by commercial traffic, as the road which it carries forms a convenient transfer between the M4 motorway and the A40. While I was admiring its design and waxing poetic about its graceful proportions a heavy eight-wheeled Continental container truck passed over. The onlookers watched with some misgivings, but had no cause to be concerned, the old bridge gallantly took the load without so much as a tremor.

When one pauses to think that our forefathers of the time could not possibly have envisaged a greater load for their structure than a heavily laden dray and several horses, one never ceases to marvel at the thoroughness of their building and the strength of their foundations.

In the morning we moved on and it was very pleasant travelling as the river wound its way through the sunlit countryside, its erratic course forming an ever changing boundary line between the counties of Berkshire and Oxford.

There was one more overnight stop before we reached Lechlade just over the border in Gloucestershire, a charming place with its mellow stone buildings and wide streets. The town played an important role in the heyday of commercial water carriage. It is recorded that a hundred barges and narrow boats could sometimes be seen tied up at its wharves and loading places. Records also tell us that stone for the dome of St. Paul's Cathedral was loaded here

Barrhead in the entrance to the Thames and Severn canal. River Thames.

Hard aground below Kempsford. River Thames.

for transport down the river. Though the customers of the May Bush Inn might hotly dispute it, the thirteenth century St. John's Bridge here was the first bridge to be put across the Thames outside London.

The next morning we took our baskets and went shopping in the town, to be jerked with brutal suddeness into the seething mechanical age that we are developing for ourselves. Heavy transport crossing from one motorway to another and the usual rash of private cars jammed the thoroughfares, making the crossing of the street with young children a hazardous business. After less than two weeks on the waterways away from the hurly-burly of the roads, when the tempo of life had been governed by the leisurely speed of the boat, the hustle and confusion in this ancient town seemed almost part of another world. It is regrettable that Lechlade and other places like it, built and developed in a quieter and infinitely more graceful age, should suffer so. Perhaps we should all step out of the rat race now and again and slow down long enough to take a hard look at the untold damage that the motor vehicle is doing to our environment.

Back on the peaceful river we slowly made our way up-stream to Inglesham. Here, hard by its confluence with the Coln, another Cotswold river, is a sight to sadden any lover of the waterways, the derelict and overgrown entrance to the disused Thames and Severn canal. The distinctive round lock-keeper's cottage and the nearby bridge are still standing, the cottage encased in ivy and the bridge almost obscured by trees and undergrowth. The lock gates themselves, probably unmoved for some sixty years, were in surprisingly good condition.

With some feelings of nostalgia we did what we had set out from Gloucester to achieve, we put the fore end of Barrhead into the overgrown entrance of the canal. Looking up the obstructed line we let our fancies take us through the lock to climb steadily up to the summit at Siddington. A leisurely run across the eight-mile pound would have brought us to the cutting at Coates. Here we would have switched on our lights to negotiate the long tunnel under Sapperton Hill. From Daneway we would have descended the beautiful Golden Valley, perhaps staying a little while in Brimscombe Port before going on to join the Stroudwater at Wallbridge.

As all this was denied us it was decided to take the boat as high up the river as possible. There has been some discussion concerning

" Will we go over or under , Mummy ? " Oxford Canal.

Jammed lower gate, Roundham Lock, Oxford Canal.

the feasibility of improving the river above Lechlade to make navigation to the new Cotswold Water Park possible. The scheme has the blessing of the Inland Waterways Association and my son and myself, as members, thought that we could obtain some useful first-hand information.

We succeeded in thrusting our way up-stream to within a mile of Kempsford church, several times grounding hard on the gravel bottom. At last we had to admit defeat when the fore end rested on a stoney bottom and the way back was barred by a large bank of gravel that had been thrown up by the screw. This had built up so high that the crew, standing in the river to clear it away, found that the water only came halfway up their calves.

The gravel cleared, Barrhead was eventually released by dint of some hard work with ropes and boathooks. As it is bad practice to run a marine gearbox for an extended period in reverse, we were faced with a 2 mile stern haul over the shoals to a place where the river was wide enough for the boat to be turned, or ' wound ' in canal parlance.

The return down-river was made in much the same unhurried fashion as the outward run, but this time we left the Thames by way of the short Duke's Cut to by-pass the city of Oxford and join the canal near the lock of this name.

The shallow Kidlington Green riser was climbed without incident but at Roundham lock we ran into trouble and suffered some delay. Going in over the bottom sill our screw churned up some rubbish and it was found impossible to close the single lower gate. After an hour or so of fruitless endeavour to clear it with inadequate tackle, the British Waterways Depot at Thrupp was telephoned. Help arrived within the space of fifteen minutes in the shape of two men and a van with suitable tools. After some trouble four large square stones were fished up with a long rake, or ' keb ', when it was found that the gate would again close. Nearby a stone cottage was being demolished and undoubtedly some young people had thought it a great joke to heave parts of the masonry into the lock chamber.

There are in existence in the canal museums some of the old notices stating clearly that the penalty for damaging canals, or their works, was deportation. No-one of course has any desire to return to justice of this severity, but it does make one wonder whether we are not looking too benignly upon vandalism and its associated sickness, the complete disregard by some members of the public for both private and community owned property.

Having duly thanked the sweating canal employees and replaced their lost liquid with mugs of cider, we worked up through the lock and resumed our travels.

Again we made only a nodding acquaintance with Banbury, preferring instead the pleasant village of Cropredy, site of a famous battle of the Civil War.

After passing Wormleighton reservoir the canal enters a straight narrow section with vertical rocky sides, the opened-out working which used to penetrate the crest of the hill and which is still known as ' The Tunnel '.

That day the boat was taken as high as Napton where she was tied up below the locks. Here she would stay for a few weeks while a busy veterinary practice and a neglected building business received some attention.

In three weeks the owners were back, bringing with them this time a miniature motor-cycle that would just fit into the boot of a car. This was to be carried on the boat as a tender and used at the last stopping place of each day to ferry someone back to the starting point to recover the car.

The evening saw us at Braunston and it was here that there was an unfortunate accident involving the dog. It happened while Barrhead was being manoeuvred and at the time no one knew he was in the water. Someone raised the alarm when he was noticed struggling in the vortex created by the propellor, which was going astern. The steerer went very smartly into neutral, but not before the poor animal was drawn near enough to the screw for the tip of a blade to sever one of his toes and a tendon.

Philip carried out the necessary first aid and at once set out with him in the car for the surgery in Gloucester, where he received expert attention. I am pleased to say that Sweep is making an excellent recovery and there are high hopes that his efficiency as a working dog will not be greatly impaired. Philip was back that night with the invalid and the next morning we travelled on to Hawkesbury Junction where the Oxford was forsaken for the Coventry canal.

In succeeding week-ends the boat was worked through this canal and through the junction at Fradley on to the Trent and Mersey. Keeping to this as far as Haywood we turned to join the northern section of the Staffs and Worcester canal. The split bridges on this

Fred, one of the last of the boat 'osses.
Gas Street Basin, Birmingham.

" Now who in the devil left a paddle up ? "

line, which enabled a tow-rope to be passed through the parapet and arch without detachment from boat or horse, was a useful and time saving innovation in the days before mechanical power came to the canals.

Our original intention was to travel on the Trent and Mersey as far as Middlewich before crossing westwards by the Shropshire Union to join the Llangollen canal.

The Trent and Mersey runs through the heart of the Potteries and traverses an area riddled by salt mines, where there has been much subsidence over the years. A new length of canal was cut some fifteen years ago to replace a bad sinkage.

Bridges and tunnels have also suffered and we had some practical experience of this about eight years ago when trying to put Venus through a bridge on the outskirts of Stoke. At the time we were pressing on in the half-light to find a suitable mooring place. The arch had dropped on one side and it was found that the saloon roof fouled by about an inch. The solution to the problem seemed to be more weight, with the only ballast available, human beings. The bridge carried a fairly busy street, so we busked the pavements above, recruiting people to come and sit in the saloon while the boat was put through. A nearby inn was just closing its doors and a windfall was provided when almost all the patrons of the public bar agreed to co-operate. Someone used his persuasive powers on the members of a waiting bus queue and this also yielded a substantial contribution. Among others a meek little man who was taking his dog for a lamp-post walk also agreed to sit in. He did however make the reservation that his wife said that he must be back in ten minutes. The volunteers, numbering about forty, most of them a little inebriated and rather noisy thought it a great joke, with the exception of the little man, who sat with his dog on his lap and kept complaining that his wife would be wondering what had happened to him. There was some bucolic singing and it was difficult to get full co-operation, but after moving the human ballast around to get the trim right the bridge was safely negotiated.

A somewhat similar experience occurred later on the same waterway when Venus this time became trapped under the subsided roof of Harecastle tunnel. This was a bad spot and at this point the towpath had been partly removed in order to give more headroom. We had been doubtful about a clear passage before we went underground but had taken the advice of a local sage who, with knees bent had squinted along the line of the saloon top and pronounced, " Aye, 'er'll go."

Venus was about in the centre of the tunnel when there was a nasty grinding noise from the fore end, unmistakable evidence that in fact, ' 'Er wouldn't go '.

After many futile attempts to reverse out of trouble we sat in the blackness and discussed ways and means of extricating the boat. Meanwhile the females aboard, with only the eerie drip of water breaking the silence, were letting their fertile imaginations run away with them. Before we could decide on a plan of action welcome lights appeared behind us. These turned out to be the headlights of a British Waterways tug which, by a great stroke of good fortune, was making her way home after a delivery commission. With the stem of the tug hard against our rudder post the engine of Venus was set at full throttle. For a full minute nothing happened while we could hear the master of the tug gradually opening up his engine. There were further grating sounds, while we held our breath wondering what was happening, before Venus passed under the obstruction and into freedom.

Out in the blessed sunlight we anxiously looked for damage. The structure of the saloon itself had stood up well to the strain, the only parts to suffer were the protecting strips of wood on the corners. These had taken all the abrasion of the tunnel masonry and were now rounded instead of square. There were some broad grins from the crew of the tug as we thanked them for their help.

The trip planned this time, to stay on the Trent and Mersey and make a circular tour taking in the Welsh canal, had to be abandoned when it was learned that repairs to Harecastle tunnel were about to be commenced and that it would be closed for several months. Instead the Shropshire Union main line was followed as far north as Hurleston Junction, where we joined the Llangollen canal. Having read much of this attractive waterway, known also as the Ellesmere or Welsh canal, we were anxious to explore its historic charms and cross the famous Pontcysyllte Aqueduct.

From the Shropshire Union proper there is a step up of four locks with a total rise of 34 ft. 3 ins. and in the first of these we again ran into a little trouble. As the chamber filled Barrhead's stem duly rose with the water level but her back end remained firmly held down by an area of jutting masonry. As the angle increased strange sounds issued from the galley as saucepans and frying pans

Exercise time.

Pontcysyllte Aqueduct, Llangollen Canal.

slithered from the cooker and shelves. Water started to run over into the rear well deck and as the boat assumed what was considered to be an unacceptable angle someone ran to drop the top paddles. Before this could be done the back of the boat suddenly leapt up about 3 ft. and the situation was relieved, but not without a certain amount of alarm.

Progress became increasingly difficult as we advanced and there were frequent stoppages when the boat grounded, or became " stemmed up ' as the old boatmen would have it. This of course was expected as a warning notice at the entrance to the canal advised that craft drawing over 2 ft. were not recommended to use the waterway. As Barrhead has a draught of 2 ft. 6 ins. it was no wonder that we were in some trouble. In one or two of the locks it had been found necessary to lift the paddles of the top gates and provide a flash of water to enable her to be brought in over the bottom sill.

There is quite a current down the canal, caused by fresh water which is passed down its whole length to feed the 85,000,000 gallon Hurleston reservoir situated near its exit into the Shropshire Union. In the narrow bridge-holes this was most apparent where Barrhead took up almost all the width of the waterway. Here she was slowed and sometimes brought to a stop when the oncoming water was unable to pass through the restricted space quickly enough and built up in the pound ahead.

Immediately after crossing the Chirk Aqueduct we entered the tunnel of the same name where we bumped rather alarmingly over the rocky bottom for most of the way.

In the Dee valley we were taken along the wooded hillside for almost a mile before the canal swept us round with exciting suddeness on to the Pontcysyllte Aqueduct. Thomas Telford's engineering masterpiece takes the canal across the valley of the Dee in a cast iron trough supported on eighteen stone pillars standing 121 ft. above the river. It is 1,007 ft. in length and crossing it was a stimulating and exciting experience. The incredibly beautiful view up the Vale of Llangollen left a memory that will last for a long time.

The farther we progressed the harder became the going and another notice advising that the canal was now only suitable for boats of 1 ft. 6 ins. draught was hardly encouraging.

The final 14 miles of the Welsh canal, without locks, crossing valleys and rivers and winding round the mountainside hundreds of feet up as it does, is a permanent testimony to Telford's consummate skill as a civil engineer.

After much physical effort and many temporary groundings we finally reached Llangollen and the heartfelt comment by one of the crew that he felt as though he had carried the boat for most of the way, did not sound too improbable. As the last $1\frac{1}{2}$ miles of this lovely waterway was literally impassable for a craft of Barrhead's size, she was turned in the ' winding hole ' at the town and left ready for the return journey.

After another week at home Jeremy with his wife and two children were back, accompanied by a young and agile grandmother to look after the latter. The passage back would be difficult for the two of them but, with repairs to the locks at Hurleston imminent, it was imperative that the boat should be out of the canal as soon as possible as this was to be closed until Christmas.

In lock transits, while Jeremy wound the paddles and Wendy closed the gates, their son Richard, who was barely four, was given the job of holding the tiller in the central position while the engine idled in gear, with the stem of the boat against the breast of the bottom gates. The central chamber of the three ' risers ' in the Grindly Brook staircase proved to be a short one, for here the rudder of the boat sat on the lock sill as it emptied. This lifted the rudder clean out of its hinges and a frightened little boy, with tears streaming down his cheeks, cried loudly for assistance. He was quickly rescued, but although the tiller was kicking about and was almost out of reach he had stuck manfully to the job, because Daddy had said that he must not let go.

The next week-end more help was forthcoming and despite being stemmed up several times the boat was worked through to the junction at Hurleston.

In succeeding week-ends she was brought down the Shropshire Union and on to the Staffs and Worcester. Approaching Kidderminster lock on this line the canal appears to terminate in a row of houses and a main road. Actually it enters a short ' tunnel ' immediately following the lock, a deep one with a 12 ft. rise. In the lock, with the chamber about half empty, it was noticed that Barrhead's fore end was holding up and that the boat was assuming an unallowable angle. The bottom paddles were quickly closed and the top ones raised to replace some of the water. An investigation showed that a 12 ft. length of 3 in. × 2 in. timber was jammed hard between the lock masonry and the hull. It took some vigorous pile driving with a hefty gangplank to free it and force it under the boat.

The Staffs and Worcester fully lived up to its reputation of being one of the most unsavoury and refuse-riddled routes of the whole canal system, for below Caldwell lock the engine suddenly pulled up without the slightest warning. The trophies retrieved from a very fouled propellor this time were a long nylon nightdress, a length of barbed wire, a fishing line and a 20 ft. length of ½ in. bore plastic tube. A sounding on the depth of water here showed no more than 2 ft. 9 ins. in the very middle and considerably less elsewhere. Further investigation in the centre of the canal disclosed that there was a good 2 ft. of soft mud above the puddle.

A few miles further on Barrhead climbed over a very solid obstruction that ground its way noisily along the bottom of the boat before finally knocking the rudder assembly out of its bottom bearing bracket.

There were no further incidents of note and that evening she was tied up in Stourport Basin to await another week-end when a crew would be available. A conversation with the foreman of the maintenance yard revealed that the dredger stationed here is only able to clear about 1½ miles of the canal in a year. Time alone will show if the battles of restoration and preservation are being won or lost on the Staffs and Worcester.

It took two more week-ends in late January for Barrhead to complete the final leg down the Severn to Gloucester. These followed a period of heavy rain with the river in flood and at its highest for many years, with water cascading over the weirs and encroaching on surrounding meadows. There was an element of danger in these conditions and great care was exercised as a 70 ft. long narrow boat, designed primarily for the still waters of the canal system, would be very vulnerable and could get completely out of control if allowed to get broadside on to a stream of this strength. No thought whatever was entertained of taking children on these occasions.

The first week-end Jeremy and Wendy left their car in Worcester and travelled to Stourport by the service bus, a journey of fifty minutes. Some idea of the fast and exhilarating return run down the swollen river may be gained by the fact that the journey to the city, a considerably greater distance than that by road, took only a matter of two and three quarter hours.

No stop was made at Diglis and they continued to Tewkesbury, where Barrhead was taken on to the Avon and moored in a quiet

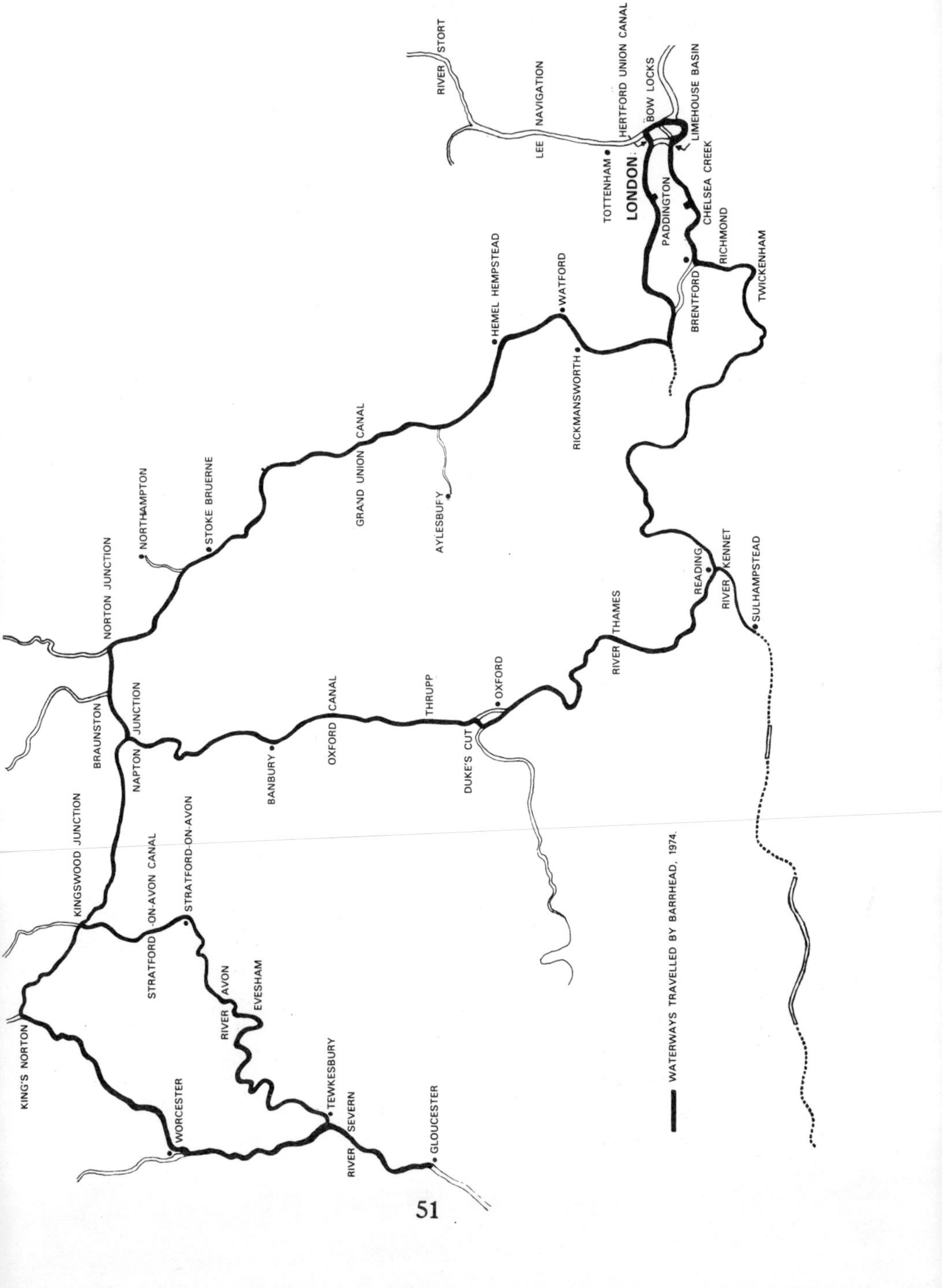
RIVER STORT
LEE NAVIGATION
HERTFORD UNION CANAL
BOW LOCKS
LIMEHOUSE BASIN
TOTTENHAM
LONDON
CHELSEA CREEK
PADDINGTON
RICHMOND
TWICKENHAM
BRENTFORD
HEMEL HEMPSTEAD
WATFORD
RICKMANSWORTH
GRAND UNION CANAL
AYLESBURY
STOKE BRUERNE
NORTHAMPTON
NORTON JUNCTION
BRAUNSTON
NAPTON JUNCTION
READING
RIVER KENNET
SULHAMPSTEAD
RIVER THAMES
OXFORD
THRUPP
OXFORD CANAL
BANBURY
DUKE'S CUT
KINGSWOOD JUNCTION
STRATFORD-ON-AVON CANAL
STRATFORD-ON-AVON
RIVER AVON
EVESHAM
KING'S NORTON
WORCESTER
TEWKESBURY
RIVER SEVERN
GLOUCESTER
WATERWAYS TRAVELLED BY BARRHEAD, 1974.

and pleasant spot away from the main stream, near the picturesque 12th century Abel Fletcher's Mill.

The next week-end some careful calculations were made before leaving Tewkesbury for the last run home. With the stream running so strongly it was thought advisable to endeavour to arrive at Gloucester at the time, or just after, when the up-coming bore had halted the flow. It is a hazardous manoeuvre getting a full length narrow boat safely into the lock entrance at the docks against the influence of a flood tide going down the weir channel.

A friend who makes a regular coal delivery down the river once came near to disaster with a fully laden narrow boat and butty. Only by some quick thinking and with the assistance of a capable and agile wife was he able to make fast and save himself and the boats from serious trouble.

At the time of this last run gales were sweeping the country and with a sou'-wester directly against the stream the river was quite choppy. It was most interesting to note the movement of the flat-bottomed craft in these conditions. There was no inclination whatever to pitch or roll, she just bounced up and down as though on a spring mattress. The gale carried the water thrown up by the blunt bows over on to the saloon top and from thence into the face of the steerer almost 70 ft. away.

At the Upper Parting it could be seen that all was well, the stream was obviously losing some strength.

On arrival at the lock entrance it was found that the tide had already turned and Barrhead was able to make a well-ordered and dignified return home. By tea-time she was safely back at her mooring in the Victoria basin.

Come the early spring she will again be taken up-river and on to the canals to explore still more of the less frequented sections of the waterway system.

It was always the intention of the publisher to include with this book a reduced copy of the large wall map, published by the British Waterways Board and showing the whole of the waterways system. The first two parts of Narrow Boat Venture had already been prepared and printed before it was known that an up-dated version of the map was in course of production. This was to include the new county boundaries, new water authority areas, more of the independent navigations and other up-datings. It is vital that any new book concerning the waterways should contain the very latest information and it was decided that publication of Narrow Boat Venture should be held back pending supplies of the new map. The opportunity thus afforded by the delay has been taken to bring the account of Barrhead's further travels up to date.

Early in 1974 the boat was put into dry-dock for inspection and repainting below the waterline. Apart from a few 'battle scars' sustained in encounters with metal objects dumped in the canals and abrasions from the rocky bottoms of some of the more shallow routes, the hull was in good condition.

Later in the year—after other maintenance work had been completed—Barrhead was again taken up-river from Gloucester with the objective this time of travelling that part of the Grand Union Canal as yet unfamiliar to the crew.

It was further planned to see a little of the Lee and Stort Navigation before exploring the routes through London and, later, as much as was navigable from the eastern end of the Kennet and Avon Canal.

The start was delayed in order that the upper Avon from Evesham to Stratford, opened by the Queen Mother on June 1st, could be used as a new through-route to Kingswood Junction.

This restoration, completed despite steeply rising costs, adds historical and interesting mileage to the cruising waterways and is a valuable addition to the pleasure amenities of the country. Dues for passage of this section are required in addition to the possession of a B.W.B. licence. The tolls are necessary to provide funds for maintenance and running expenses, as this is an independent waterway, administered by the Upper Avon Navigation Trust.

Perhaps it is a good thing for all of us to be reminded sometimes of the extensive cruising waters, the mooring facilities, refuse and sewage disposal points and other services available to holders of a B.W.B. licence, and of the excellent value we receive for our money.

The canals from Kingswood to Braunston Junction were familiar to the crew and passage of them has been described earlier in the story, but south of the latter we were on new water.

Hereabouts we made friends with the crew of a commercial boat and worked up the Braunston flight 'breasted up' to their craft, a motor narrow boat owned by Union Canal Carriers Ltd. The men were most helpful and suggested that we might stop our engine. We, for our part, were perfectly happy to become their butty for the time being. A stop for the night was made at Buckby top lock and a convivial evening spent with our travelling companions in the bar of the New Inn, conveniently situated at the lock side.

From here on it was quiet travelling through pleasant countryside, with few locks.

At Weedon we were jerked back to the realities of the present age and our soliloquies brought to an abrupt conclusion. Here there is an intermingling of all the main elements of our transport system, with the A.5., developed from what was a Roman road, the canal, a busy main line railway and the M.1. motorway in close proximity. Needless to say the scene is not one of peace and tranquillity.

Blisworth Tunnel fully lived up to its reputation of being one of the wettest in the country. Built—like all our canal tunnels—without foresight that power would some day come to the waterways, its ventilation also cannot apparently cope with the exhaust from even a moderate volume of traffic, for it was full of smoke. Philip, who was steering, proceeded with no confidence at all after striking the side-walls several times; with the headlights of the boat obscured in smoke some 70 ft. away one can lose all sense of direction. Luckily, the headlights of approaching craft could just be discerned at the last moment and three of these were passed carefully without incident.

A most absorbing time was spent at the Stoke Bruerne Museum, our enjoyment marred a little by efforts to maintain order and quiet among four healthy and inquisitive children.

We had learned of the temporary water shortage being experienced on this section and were surprised by the refusal of other boats' crews to share locks with us.

The hire companies we were told had strongly advised against the practice, presumably to lessen the risk of damage to their boats. Some of the pounds were rather low and we waited at the head of one lock for a hire boat whose crew appeared to be having trouble in preparing the chamber. Our offer of help was tartly refused so we all retired below for coffee.

Ten minutes later Barrhead grounded firmly on the mud, the cause—as was suspected— a paddle in the lower gate not fully closed. We were stung into making a succinct reply when the crew of the other boat complained that they could not leave the lock because we were blocking the cut. Fortunately it was a short pound and the matter was rectified without a too serious loss of water. I hasten to add that an instance such as this is an isolated case. We have always found the great majority of boat hirers to be courteous and friendly, responsible people who also have a real interest in the canals.

The passage of the Ouse Aqueduct attracted everyone's interest and would have undoubtedly impressed us more had we not crossed the spectacular Pontcysyllte first.

At Soulbury we waited at the tail of the three locks while three small cruisers were put through in turn. We entered into conversation with the crews but hesitated this time before attempting to offer any advice. Jeremy and Philip finally gave up trying to convince them that they were wasting water and retired in frustration to the near-by inn.

We went on to climb the Marsworth flight, assisted with the paddles by a co-operative lockeeper.

The summit pound was exceptionally low—the level 18 ins. below normal ; it was slow going but we experienced no trouble.

At Berkhamstead it became apparent that the canal was now in the outer fringes of the Capital, industry was well established and there was little open country to be seen.

The passing of Cassiobury Park provided a welcome change.

Water levels were now at weir-height and we met several large canal barges looking high and wide in the confined waters.

Came Sunday evening and the boat was left at Rickmansworth where she was originally registered.

The next week-end Barrhead was moved on and moored in the basin at Little Venice, where some of the crew would stay for several days. The opportunity was taken—among other things—of visiting the British Museum, where the junior members had a thrilling time in the children's section, pressing the buttons and making all their science fiction stories come true.

Later in the week the boat was taken on to a mooring near the London Zoo where they were further able to enjoy themselves.

The Regent's Park Canal provides firm evidence that even an urban waterway can still be a dignified and pleasant thoroughfare. The cut was deep and wide and Barrhead ran freely and without wash. There was, however, an incredible amount of floating timber in it, so much in fact that B.W.B. maintain a special boat with a hydraulic scoop to retrieve it.

So often the cities and towns present their disreputable backsides to the canal and an entirely wrong impression of the place can be given to the traveller on the waterway.

Perhaps this is something to which local authorities should give thought. The recent article on British canals published in the Geographical Magazine has stimulated great interest in our waterways, particularly in the U.S.A. We have already met one of what may be many future visitors from the country to holiday on our canals.

At Old Ford Locks the man in charge advised us to go through the Hertford Union Canal and so to the river Lee in order to enter the Thames at Bow Locks.

We were now short of time and were obliged to abandon our plan to explore more of the river Lee. It had been our original intention to lock out at Limehouse Basin but the lock here is only operative for three hours preceding high water, while that at Bow is open for two hours after in addition. Passing on down 'Duckett's Cut', as the Hertford Union is affectionately known, we entered the Lee. The river in these lower reaches is essentially commercial and cannot be recommended for lightly-built pleasure craft. Much of the traffic consists of large swim-ended Thames lighters towed by small (40 ft.) tugs. The lighters are not steered and consequently swing alarmingly wide on the many sharp bends.

At Bow Locks the Lee becomes tidal and is known as Bow Creek. Here, there was a most trying and aggravating delay of two hours while an over-zealous official held us in the large lock while he checked the licence. We eventually persuaded him to telephone the Watford headquarters of the B.W.B., when he had to reluctantly agree that everything was in order. Without this delay our timing would have been quite satisfactory. We would have been obliged to 'punch the tide' in Bow Creek but would have had the benefit of the Thames flow up through the city.

As it was we did not leave Bow Locks till an hour or so after high water, in company with a tug and its lighter.

Released from bondage and preceded by the other craft, we fairly flew down the two miles-long, tortuous, muddy creek and shot out into the broad waters of the Thames like a cork out of a bottle, or so it seemed.

The tug with its lighter skidded off down-river on the strong ebb with the skipper waving his arms to attract our attention and pointing vigorously up-stream. Jeremy, who was steering, just had time to recover from his surprise and collect his wits before taking action to prevent us from being swept on to a large mooring buoy, almost as big as Barrhead. The buoy, straining at its cable was showing an impressive ' bow wave ' and though our engine was at full throttle, equivalent to 7 knots over the ground, we did not appear to be gaining on it. We were not in real danger, but the narrow boat was out of her element in these conditions and any false move or misjudgement could have put us at hazard. It was as well that Jeremy—quite experienced in conditions such as these—was in charge for, as it proved later, the situation required some decisive thinking and good boat handling. Even he had to admit that he was scared at times.

By moving as close inshore as possible we found that we could make some progress.

It was Saturday and the river looked like a busy street with the pleasure steamers, together with the larger commercial craft, taking advantage of the ebb tide. There were two separate two-way traffic systems, with the large freighters in the middle, tugs, pleasure steamers and the like on either side and lines of moored lighters—like taxi ranks—on the outside. We crept along between the lighters and the shore.

As the river swept round a long bend we found ourselves travelling much further than we cared for.

Taking his courage in both hands Jeremy waited for the traffic to thin out and crossed to the other side. We were about in the middle of the main shipping lane when a hovercraft appeared from nowhere and roared past. As it left the water it raised a large wave and this, after a few seconds, was straddled by Barrhead. The children, for safety reasons, were confined below with mothers to look after them. Almost immediately the anxious face of one of the girls appeared to enquire what the strange creaking noises had been. There had obviously been some structural movement, but as an unconverted narrow boat hull has comparatively little lateral rigidity it speaks well for the construction of the superstructure that it stood up to this sort of punishment.

Once on the other side of the river progress improved greatly, the current being much weaker on the inside of the bend.

Here there was a lot to be seen, many docks and much shipping tied up to the wharves.

The river now swung right-handed so we decided to change sides again. Jeremy had almost completed the manoeuvre when the boat

Barrhead clearing Tower Bridge, River Thames.

Passing the replica of the Golden Hind, River Thames.

was again caught in rough water. We had a big tanker to port of us and a hovercraft coming up astern.

Just as we were about to ride the tanker's wash the hovercraft took off, setting up a rolling wave that added further confusion to the water ahead of us. Jeremy turned into the biggest waves and hoped for the best. Our blunt fore-end hit them with a hearty smack and disappeared into a cloud of flying water. Barrhead pitched forward alarmingly and the engine raced away as the propellor came out of the river. There were cries of alarm from below and we could hear the sound of breaking crockery and the clatter of cooking pans as they slithered to the floor of the galley.

Once through the broken water, we lost no time in regaining our refuge behind the lines of moored lighters. It was plainly apparent—if indeed we needed further convincing—that flat bottomed narrow boats are definitely not suitable for these conditions. We seriously considered tying up to a moored lighter to await the turn of the tide but decided that it was better to 'stick with the devil that we knew' and at least retain some freedom of action.

Above Limehouse Basin the river becomes narrower and the current consequently stronger. Avoiding the main arch of Tower Bridge we went through a side span where the current intensified and we made very little headway.

The pleasure steamers all made about 12 knots and appeared to have their own 'rules of the road'. Jeremy decided that it was better to plough straight on and let them avoid us—it seemed to work, but earned us some funny looks. Let us trust that this was solely due to the strange appearance of a gaily painted narrow boat in the tideway.

With less shipping and better conditions we were feeling more relaxed and pictures were taken of the cruiser Belfast, the Houses of Parliament and other sights. It is unfortunate that we do not have pictures of Barrhead taken at the time of her more violent antics but at that moment everyone was much too concerned with safety to take photographs.

The traffic gradually thinned out and in an effort to escape the worst of the stream the boat was taken so far inshore that we had to move out periodically to avoid pipe out-falls and the like. A police launch passed and called us on the loud hailer, "It's shallow there". The steerer thanked them and shouted a reply that it was deep enough for us.

There were many houseboats tied up on the mud above Chelsea Creek.

Passing Brentford we noted the large number of barges and lighters moored outside the entrance to the Grand Union Canal.

Approaching Richmond we did at last run aground. The boat pulled up gradually before sliding gently off the mud into the centre of the river. Checking the depth we found that it was even less than 3 ft. in the middle. As this was still plenty for us we pressed on and reached the lock. This, we were relieved to find, was open and after several tussles with the mud at its entrance we finally made it into the chamber. No inspection was required and after paying a very moderate toll we were allowed to re-fill our water tank at no extra charge. After enquiries as to the best shops and pub, we asked about moorings. The lockeeper informed us that the level below the lock would dry out even more and advised mooring under the railway bridge, adding that the river would top the weir by about 3 ft. at high water, then return to normal level some time during the night.

Moving up to the bridge we tied up—leaving plenty of slack on our mooring ropes.

The noise here was continuous and un-nerving, a far, far cry from the peace of a rural canal. Traffic on a busy road, a steel bridge carrying commuter trains every three minutes and the incessant sound of low-flying aircraft made sleep almost impossible.

There was ample time to reflect upon the happenings of an eventful day with some sense of achievement ; Regent's Park to Richmond would be good going under any conditions.

The next day we moved on to Teddington where we left Port of London Authority waters and entered those of the Thames Conservancy. It was quite a pleasant change to have the locks operated for us. The over-development of the land around the river was not to our taste but we had a comfortable run to Reading.

Here, we turned on to the Kennet, the junction of the rivers dominated by the gas works and the backs of red-brick houses.

The first lock is Thames Conservancy though we operated this ourselves. Passing through the narrow tortuous passage by the brewery we gradually left the town behind and continued to Burghfield, where the boat was to be left for a time.

One week-end a little later—while the boat stayed where she was—some of us decided to take another look at that most interesting section of the derelict Thames and Severn Canal, from

Chalford to the summit level at Daneway. The tow-path, the passage of which at one time more resembled a trek through the jungle, is now a civilised walk.

This is entirely due to the efforts of the Stroudwater Canal Society and their helpers. Overgrowth has been cut back, the tow-path repaired and gravelled in places and sections of the bank improved and tidied. This stretch through the Golden Valley, terminating in the long Sapperton Tunnel through the Cotswolds , could be the most attractive cruising route in the country. The remoteness and tranquillity of the lovely valley through which it passes would be a perfect antidote to the hurly-burly of city life and the pressures of modern business. Perhaps I may be forgiven for a little bias in this respect for I was born within sight of the canal a little after the turn of the century, when a few trows still came up from the Severn and narrowboats went through the tunnel to the Thames and London.

It can be stated with confidence that there is no great physical obstacle to the restoration of this part of the waterway.

The Stroudwater Canal Society, soon to become (it is hoped) the Stroudwater, Thames and Severn Canal Trust Ltd., has recently carried out a detailed survey on the tunnel.

Seven members, using four small boats and led by a professional civil engineer, have reported that much of the lining is in excellent condition and that, despite one bad fall and several less severe, the clearance and restoration of this, the second longest canal tunnel in the country, is a more feasible proposition than has hitherto been thought. There are of course other technical difficulties, none of which are incapable of being surmounted by modern equipment and materials.

The diminutive wharf at Chalford was the base of the small fleet of narrow boats operated by the late James Smart, and then by his son Harry, now also passed to the place where all good boatmen go. Recently some old documents of the business have been resurrected, among them several letters from the masters of the boats. These are now in the archives of the County Records Office at Gloucester and a perusal of them is both fascinating and enlightening. The main theme of them all seems to be the request for cash to be forwarded, as witness the following.

> dear sir I write to inform you that we shall finish loading today friday middle day we hope to get up the river saturday Harry is not got down here i suppose he is frose up in the canal we have got

a good load please to send one pound by return of post to post office Abingdon by return yours of haste ______

The boatmen had no time for such superfluities as capitals and punctuation marks but they were required to act very much on their own initiative in securing freight for their boats, as is shown by the following letter, posted from Gloucester in 1886.

sir just a line to let you know that we have got all the timber from Wainlode hill and its not much more than one boat load and we have been to hempstad bridge and thare is not much thare and that wot is thare is all top as harry took all the big. we have heared that there is ten tons of slate at prices [Price's Yard] and we are going to have that on if we can find a nough to make a load we are going to stop and have it all at present yours truely __

One can almost feel the presence of these honest and trusted servants of the little carrying company in a walk along the deserted and silent line of the old canal.

Restoration of the waterway from Chalford to Stroud is a different and much more difficult problem, with a factory, a car park, various roads and an unsightly industrial dump completely obliterating the original line. Much work has already been done in this section and the Society is confident that even the formidable obstacles mentioned can be overcome, or by-passed, provided that adequate funds are forthcoming.

A few weeks later some of the crew of Barrhead were back again at Burghfield, at a time of gales and torrential rains. The Kennet was swollen and running fast. Moving on to the limit of navigation at Sulhampstead was hard work in the teeth of the wind and against the current. The return down-stream with the gale behind was quite exhilarating and the only problem that of stopping the boat. On one particularly bad bend Barrhead went out of control for the only time in our experience. Assailed by a fierce gust broadside on she hit the bank with a hefty thump. To add to the commotion the overhanging branch of a tree broke the ¼" plate glass window of a cabin. Even all this confusion was not enough to wake two year-old Helen who slept serenely through it all in the bunk below.

Many trees were blown down, some of them partly into the river, but we were not impeded and the Thames was reached without further incident.

The countryside gradually becomes more rural above Reading and we had a pleasant run to Oxford. No one was anxious to repeat the ‘ ditch crawl ’ through the city that was experienced the previous year so the boat was taken up to Godstow Lock and through Duke’s Cut to the Oxford Canal, the next stop being made at Thrupp.

The next week-end she was again taken north. From here it was steady canal travelling at 4 m.p.h. with ample time to enjoy the unfolding Oxfordshire countryside.

On subsequent week-ends, as time and business allowed, the boat was worked through to Worcester by various combinations of crew, sometimes accompanied by friends, over familiar waters already described earlier.

With the Severn on its best behaviour she returned to Gloucester without any further incident of note.

In 1975 it is the owners’ intention to visit and explore more of the waterways in the north of the country.